Warm Hats for WEE NOGGINS

These little knitted hats provide big warmth for premature, newborn, and larger babies!
Keeping babies warm is so important to their health! That's why Glenna Anderson Muse designed these hats for babies in the hospital where she works. The sweet seasonal patterns are specially sized for Small to Large Preemie babies and also include Term sizes (newborn to 12 months) so that every baby can have a cozy cap. Each design is based on one of four basic hat styles—and they look just as adorable without a holiday theme.
Don't miss this exciting opportunity to turn your knitting into gifts of love for the babies who need them!

Meet the Designer

Hi. I'm a respiratory therapist in Springfield, Missouri. I work in adult care, NICU (Neonatal Intensive Care Unit), and pediatrics. For three years, I have been creating patterns for the "little-Littles" in our NICU. I'm also a member of a knitting group that stocks our NICU with hats, booties, and cuddling blankets.

My personal area of expertise is creating themed hats that we send home with our babies as souvenirs of their time with us.

Knitting these hats became a mission for me when the mother of a 25-week, 24-ounce baby said, "On Easter morning, I saw the bunny ears on my baby's head and smiled. For the first time, I felt hope she would come home. I love how your hats make me feel my baby is real!"

A smile may seem like a small thing to you and me, but I am humbled and grateful to be a part of a project that can bring a smile to someone who lives in fear of losing a child.

A note on the sillier hats: I've delighted in each turkey, reindeer, and pumpkin hat I've knitted and put on those little-Little heads. However, I ran into one objection along the way—from my husband! While looking at a reindeer hat on my doll model, he laughed and said, "You know one day these little guys are going to grow up, form a mob, and kick your behind for making them look silly, right?" I just smiled and said, "As long as they **grow up**, I'd be happy for them to complain."

I would like to dedicate this collection to my mother for teaching me knitting and the blessing of giving; my husband for patiently and passionately supporting me; and the doctors, nurses, respiratory therapists, educators, nurses' aides, and unit secretaries who make the NICU of Cox South Hospital a place of miracles.

— Glenna Anderson Muse

Table of Contents

LEISURE ARTS, INC.
Little Rock, Arkansas

NOTES FROM GLENNA

How a Hat Helps

Over 600,000 premature babies are born every year in the United States alone, finding themselves in NICUs (Neonatal Intensive Care Units) with their anxious parents nearby. Premature babies need careful monitoring of their development to insure safe passage past their due dates: namely the transition of their lung development, learning to feed, and regulating their own body temperature. Even inside incubators, many babies still lose too much of their own body heat in those crucial first weeks, so a covered head is often standard operating procedure in the NICU.

While hats for full-term newborns are widely available both commercially and in needlework pattern books, the same is not true for premature babies. The lack of existing books is the reason I first began creating my own designs which, to my pleasure, became so popular with the parents and our staff that I've often been asked to resize the designs for term babies, too.

Let's Knit! Colors and Yarns

I love bright colors on babies because, from working with these little-Littles, I'm often amazed by how individual their personalities already are both at term and also at 24-36 weeks when they're still supposed to be "in the oven." The cliché of a sweet, quiet, cooing baby is not always true. While some are passive and quiet, others are feisty and moody and, quite frankly, ticked off to be out in the world early. I often choose rich, vivid, full-of-life colors to match our lively babies.

When it comes to yarn, three things should determine your choice—texture, washability, and affordability.

Due to allergic reactions with animal-based yarns, only use the softest of acrylic, bamboo, and cotton yarns for babies. While all babies have fresh new skin, premature babies can have skin that may not be completely developed yet, so any abrasive textures can be uncomfortable to them. Carefully feel the yarn you like. If it feels wonderfully soft and silky to you, then the little-Littles will like it too.

Each of the yarns used in the collection meet all three criteria. They have soft baby-friendly textures, are easily washable and re-washable, and can easily be purchased at a variety of craft stores nationwide.

Knitting Techniques Explained

CASTING ON

Casting on over two needles creates a less tightly weaved edging with more stretch and flexibility. To accomplish, simply hold the two needles side by side and cast on as if only one needle were present. Then, remove one needle and begin the project.

To use with double-pointed needles, use the same method, except place needle point protectors on each end of each needle until you pull the second needle out after casting on. The stitches will be loose and this will prevent them from slipping off the needles before you can knit around that first row.

ADDING NEW COLORS IN STRIPES

My aunt, Susan Meadows, came up with this technique: When adding a new color for a stripe, instead of letting the loose end dangle, pick it up on the second stitch knitted along with the main strand and knit several stitches using both. Then drop the loose end again and trim it on the back side. This insures a tight weave with little possibility of the loose end unraveling, plus it cuts down on the number of threads you have to weave in at the end. This is always a bonus, because isn't weaving in loose ends the least fun part of any project?

BLOCKING

I don't use a traditional block on the baby hats, although I do go over certain things like the witch's hat brim with a travel steamer to unfurl the curl. I use the lowest heat setting several inches away from the project. Another option is to lay the hat out flat, cover with a damp cloth, and press very lightly with an iron on the lowest setting. It may take a little while, so be patient. The stitches will flatten a little, but for things like uncurling leaf edges or ruffled hat edges, it's needed to get the right drape.

Sizing

Preemie:
    Small [up to 2.5 lbs (1.14 kg)]
    Medium [2.5-4 lbs (1.14-1.82 kg)]
    Large [4-6 lbs (1.82-2.72 kg)]
Term:
    Small - Newborn
    Medium - 3-6 months
    Large - 12 months

Size Note: All instructions are written with Preemie sizes Small, Medium, and Large in the first set of braces { } and with Term sizes Newborn, 3 to 6 months, and 12 months in the second set of braces. Instructions will be easier to read if you circle all the numbers pertaining to your size. If only one number is given, it applies to all sizes.

Where to Donate Your Hats

To find out where your hand-knitted hats are needed, contact the hospitals, health clinics, or social service agencies in your area.

You can also visit Care Wear Volunteers (carewear.org) to find hundreds of hospitals and agencies across the nation that may need baby hats. Be sure to read the latest Care Wear newsletter for updates.

Interested in working with other knitting volunteers? Area chapters of Newborns in Need (newbornsinneed.org) are responsible for making and distributing handmade items for babies in their local communities.

BASIC PAPER BAG HAT

This is an easy hat that comes together quickly by knitting a rectangle, seaming the short ends, and gathering the top edge with a coordinating ribbon.

++

Finished Head Circumference: {9-10-11} {12-14-16}"/{23-25.5-28}{30.5-35.5-40.5} cm
See Sizing, page 3.

MATERIALS

Medium Weight Yarn
[4 ounces, 232 yards
(113 grams, 212 meters) per skein]:
   One skein
Straight knitting needles, size 7 (4.5 mm) **or** size
   needed for gauge
$^1/_4$" (7 mm) wide washable fabric ribbon -
   18" (45.5 cm) (optional)
Yarn needle

GAUGE: In Garter Stitch (knit every row),
         18 sts and 34 rows = 4" (10 cm)

BODY

Note: Each row is worked across height of Hat.

Cast on {24-26-30}{35-40-43} sts over
2 needles *(Fig. A)*.

Fig. A

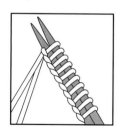

Remove one needle and work in Garter
Stitch (knit each row) until piece measures
approximately {9-10-11}{12-14-16}"/
{23-25.5-28}{30.5-35.5-40.5} cm
from cast on edge.

Bind off all sts in **knit**, leaving a long end for sewing.

FINISHING

Thread yarn needle with long end and matching cast on edge with bind off edge, sew seam.

Thread yarn needle with an 18" (45.5 cm) length of yarn. Weave needle through stitches {$^3/_4$-$^3/_4$-1} {$1^1/_4$-$1^1/_4$-$1^1/_2$}"/{2-2-2.5}{3-3-4} cm down from one edge; pull ends tightly to close top and secure with a double knot.

Optional: Thread yarn needle with ribbon. Weave needle through stitches, {$^3/_4$-$^3/_4$-1} {$1^1/_4$-$1^1/_4$-$1^1/_2$}"/{2-2-2.5}{3-3-4} cm down from one edge; pull ends tightly to close top and secure in a double knot, then tie into a bow.

Fold bottom edge up to form cuff.

HAVE A HEART

A country-style patchwork heart embellishes this quick and easy paper bag-style hat.

◼◼◻◻ EASY

Finished Head Circumference: {9-10-11} {12-14-16}"/{23-25.5-28} {30.5-35.5-40.5} cm
See Sizing, page 3.

MATERIALS

Medium Weight Yarn
[6 ounces, 335 yards (170 grams, 306 meters) per skein]:
  Ecru - One skein
  Red - small amount
Straight knitting needles, size 8 (5 mm) **or** size needed for gauge
Polyester fiberfill - small amount for Heart
Yarn needle

GAUGE: In Garter Stitch (knit every row),
      18 sts and 34 rows = 4" (10 cm)

Techniques used:
• Increase *(Figs. 2a & b, page 34)*
• K2 tog *(Fig. 3, page 34)*

BODY

With Ecru, work same as Basic Paper Bag Hat, page 4.

HEART

With Red, cast on 3 sts.

Row 1: Increase, K1, increase: 5 sts.

Row 2: Increase, K3, increase: 7 sts.

Row 3: K6, increase: 8 sts.

Row 4: Increase, K7: 9 sts.

Row 5: K8, increase: 10 sts.

Row 6: Increase, K9: 11 sts.

Row 7: K2 tog, K8, increase.

Row 8: Increase, K8, K2 tog.

Row 9: K2 tog, K8, increase.

Row 10: Knit across.

Rows 11 and 12: Repeat Rows 8 and 9.

Row 13: K9, K2 tog: 10 sts.

Row 14: K2 tog, K8: 9 sts.

Row 15: K7, K2 tog: 8 sts.

Row 16: K2 tog, K6: 7 sts.

Row 17: K2 tog, K3, K2 tog: 5 sts.

Row 18: K2 tog, K1, K2 tog: 3 sts.

Bind off all sts in **knit**, leaving a long end for sewing.

Thread needle with long end and sew Heart to center front of Hat, stuffing lightly before closing.

POSEY

Based on the Basic Paper Bag Hat design, this is a feminine celebration of spring with a top-knot flower and leaves.

■■■□□ **EASY**

Finished Head Circumference: {9-10-11}{12-14-16}"/{23-25.5-28}{30.5-35.5-40.5} cm
See Sizing, page 3.

MATERIALS

Medium Weight Yarn
[3.5 ounces, 164 yards
(100 grams, 150 meters) per skein]:
  Purple, Green, **and** Pink - One skein **each** color
Straight knitting needles, size 8 (5 mm) **or** size needed for gauge
³/₈" (10 mm) wide washable fabric ribbon - 18" (45.5 cm) (optional)
Yarn needle

GAUGE: In Garter Stitch (knit every row),
18 sts and 34 rows = 4" (10 cm)

Techniques used:
• Increase *(Figs. 2a & b, page 34)*
• K2 tog *(Fig. 3, page 34)*

BODY

Note: Each row is worked across height of Hat.

With Purple, cast on {20-22-24}{30-34-36} sts over 2 needles *(Fig. A, page 4)*.

Remove one needle and work in Garter Stitch (knit each row) until piece measures approximately {9-10-11}{12-14-16}"/{23-25.5-28}{30.5-35.5-40.5} cm from cast on edge.

Bind off all sts in **knit**, leaving a long for sewing.

POSEY

With Pink, pick up 25 sts along either long edge *(Fig. 6, page 35)*.

Row 1 (Increase row): Increase, (K1, increase) across: 38 sts.

Row 2 (Right side): Purl across.

Row 3: (Increase, K1) across: 57 sts.

Row 4: Purl across.

Rows 5 and 6: Repeat Rows 1 and 2: 86 sts.

Bind off all sts in **knit**.

LEAF (Make 2)

With Green and leaving long end for sewing, cast on 3 sts.

Row 1: Increase, K1, increase: 5 sts.

Row 2: K2, P1, K2.

Row 3: Increase, K3, increase: 7 sts.

Row 4: K3, P1, K3.

Row 5: Knit across.

Rows 6-11: Repeat Rows 4 and 5, 3 times.

Row 12: K2 tog, K3, K2 tog: 5 sts.

Row 13: K2, P1, K2.

Row 14: K2 tog, K1, K2 tog: 3 sts.

Row 15: K1, P1, K1.

Row 16: K2 tog, K1: 2 sts.

Row 17: K2 tog: one st.

Cut yarn, pull end through last st.

FINISHING

Thread yarn needle with long end on Body and matching cast on edge with bound off edge, sew seam.

Thread yarn needle with an 18" (45.5 cm) length of yarn. Weave needle through sts at base of Posey, pull ends tightly to close top and secure in a double knot, then weave in ends.

Optional: Thread yarn needle with ribbon. Weave needle through sts at base of Posey, pull ends tightly to close top and secure in a double knot, then tie into a double-knotted bow.

Thread yarn needle with long end of Leaf; sew Leaves to Hat on each side of Posey.

Fold bottom edge up to form cuff.

BASIC JESTER

This is a quick-to-knit two-needle design with simp[le] seams, creating a hat that's sure to make you smile.

◖◼◻◻ **EASY**

Finished Head Circumference: {9-10-11} {12-14-16}"/{23-25.5-28}{30.5-35.5-40.5} cm See Sizing, page 3.

MATERIALS
Medium Weight Yarn
[4 ounces, 232 yards
(113 grams, 212 meters) per skein]:
    One skein
Straight knitting needles, size 8 (5 mm) **or** size
    needed for gauge
Yarn needle

GAUGE: In Stockinette Stitch
        (knit one row, purl one row),
        16 sts and 24 rows = 4" (10 cm)

Techniques used:
• Increase *(Figs. 2a & b, page 34)*
• P2 tog *(Fig. 4, page 35)*

FRONT BOTTOM RIBBING
Cast on {20-20-24}{24-28-32} sts.

Rows 1-6: (K2, P2) across.

BODY
Increase Row: Knit across increasing
{0-2-0}{2-2-2} sts *(see Zeros, page 34)*
evenly spaced across *(see Increasing Evenly
Across, page 34)*: {20-22-24}{26-30-34} sts.

Beginning with a **purl** row, work in Stockinette Stitch (purl one row, knit one row) until piece measures approximately {8-9-11}{12-14-16}"/ {20.5-23-28}{30.5-35.5-40.5} cm from cast on edge, ending by working a **knit** row.

Decrease Row: Purl across decreasing {0-2-0} {2-2-2} sts evenly spaced across *(see Decreasing Evenly Across, page 34)*: {20-20-24}{24-28-32} sts.

BACK BOTTOM RIBBING
Rows 1-6: (K2, P2) across.

Bind off all sts **loosely** in ribbing.

FINISHING

With **wrong** side together, fold piece in half matching ribbing. Weave side seams *(Fig. 7, page 35)*.

Make 2 Tassels *(Figs. A & B)*.

Attach one Tassel to each top corner.

TASSEL

Cut a piece of cardboard 3" (7.5 cm) wide and as long as you want your finished tassel to be. Wind a double strand of yarn around the cardboard approximately 12 times. Cut an 18" (45.5 cm) length of yarn and insert it under all of the strands at the top of the cardboard; pull up tightly and tie securely. Leave the yarn ends long enough to attach the tassel. Cut the yarn at the opposite end of the cardboard and then remove it *(Fig. A)*. Cut a 6" (15 cm) length of yarn and wrap it tightly around the tassel twice, 1" (2.5 cm) below the top *(Fig. B)*; tie securely. Trim the ends.

Fig. A

Fig. B

LITTLE FRANKIE STEIN

What's more fitting for a classic Halloween than baby's first Frankenstein, or in this case, Little Frankie Stein hat?

■■□□ EASY

Finished Head Circumference:
{9-10-11}{12-14-16}"/{23-25.5-28}
{30.5-35.5-40.5} cm
See Sizing, page 3.

MATERIALS

Medium Weight Yarn 🔵**4**
[7 ounces, 355 yards
(199 grams, 325 meters) per skein]:
    Black **and** Green - One skein **each** color
    Orange - small amount
Straight knitting needles, size 8 (5 mm) **or** size
    needed for gauge
10 mm Pom-poms or buttons - 2 for eyes
Sewing needle and matching thread
Yarn needle

GAUGE: In Stockinette Stitch
      (knit one row, purl one row),
      16 sts and 24 rows = 4" (10 cm)

Techniques used:
• Increase *(Figs. 2a & b, page 34)*
• P2 tog *(Fig. 4, page 35)*

Instructions continued on page 10.

FRONT BOTTOM RIBBING

With Green, cast on {20-20-24}{24-28-32} sts.

Rows 1-6: (K2, P2) across.

BODY

Increase Row: Knit across increasing {0-2-0} {2-2-2} sts *(see Zeros, page 34)* evenly spaced across *(see Increasing Evenly Across, page 34)*: {20-22-24} {26-30-34} sts.

Beginning with a **purl** row, work in Stockinette Stitch (purl one row, knit one row) until piece measures approximately {3-3$^{1}/_{2}$-4}{4$^{1}/_{2}$-5-5$^{1}/_{2}$}"/ {7.5-9-10}{11.5-12.5-14} cm from cast on edge, ending by working a **purl** row.

Next Row: K1, with Black K1 *(Figs. 5a & b, page 35)*, (with Green K1, with Black K1) across, cut Green.

Work in Stockinette Stitch until piece measures approximately {8-9-11}{12-14-16}"/{20.5-23-28} {30.5-35.5-40.5} cm from cast on edge, ending by working a **knit** row; cut Black.

Decrease Row: With Green, purl across decreasing {0-2-0}{2-2-2} sts evenly spaced across *(see Decreasing Evenly Across, page 34)*: {20-20-24} {24-28-32} sts.

BACK BOTTOM RIBBING

Rows 1-6: (K2, P2) across.

Bind off all sts **loosely** in ribbing.

FINISHING

Please take caution when using pom-poms or buttons as they may present a choking hazard for infants and small children.

With **wrong** side together, fold piece in half. Weave side seams *(Fig. 7, page 34)*.

Using photo as a guide for placement:
With sewing needle and thread, sew pom-poms for eyes to front $^{1}/_{2}$" (12 mm) down from hair line and $^{3}/_{8}$" (10 mm) apart for eyes.
With Orange and using straight stitch *(Fig. A)*, embroider mouth below eyes.
With Black and using straight stitch, embroider scar to left of the eyes and mouth.

STRAIGHT STITCH

Straight Stitch is just what the name implies, a single, straight stitch. Come up at 1 and go down at 2.

Fig. A

SPRINGY CURLS

Quick-to-knit on two needles, the light colors and cotton give baby an extra touch of warmth on cooler days and evenings.

▰▰▰▱▱ EASY

Finished Head Circumference: {9-10-11} {12-14-16}"/{23-25.5-28}{30.5-35.5-40.5} cm
See Sizing, page 3.

MATERIALS

MEDIUM 4

Medium Weight Yarn
[3.5 ounces, 171 yards
(100 grams, 156 meters) per skein]:
    White **and** Blue - One **skein** each color
Straight knitting needles, size 8 (5 mm) **or** size
    needed for gauge
Yarn needle

GAUGE: In Stockinette Stitch
            (knit one row, purl one row),
            16 sts and 24 rows = 4" (10 cm)

Techniques used:
• Increase *(Figs. 2a & b, page 34)*
• P2 tog *(Fig. 4, page 35)*

FRONT BOTTOM RIBBING

With White, cast on {20-20-24}{24-28-32} sts.

Rows 1-6: (K2, P2) across.

BODY

Row 1 (Right side): Knit across increasing {0-2-0}{2-2-2} sts *(see Zeros, page 34)* evenly spaced across *(see Increasing Evenly Across, page 34)*: {20-22-24}{26-30-34} sts.

Row 2: Purl across.

Row 3: With Blue, knit across.

Row 4: Purl across.

Rows 5 and 6: With White, repeat Rows 3 and 4.

Rows 7-12: With Blue, repeat Rows 3 and 4, 3 times.

Rows 13-16: Repeat Rows 5-8.

Cut Blue.

Beginning with a **knit** row, work in Stockinette Stitch until piece measures approximately {5^1/$_2$-6^1/$_2$-8^1/$_2$}{9^1/$_2$-11^1/$_2$-13^1/$_2$}"/ {14-16.5-21.5}{24-29-34.5} cm from cast on edge, ending by working a **purl** row.

Next 14 Rows: Repeat Rows 3-16.

Cut Blue.

Next Row: Knit across.

Decrease Row: Purl across decreasing {0-2-0}{2-2-2} sts evenly spaced across *(see Decreasing Evenly Across, page 34)*: {20-20-24}{24-28-32} sts.

BACK BOTTOM RIBBING

Rows 1-6: (K2, P2) across.

Bind off all sts **loosely** in ribbing.

FINISHING

With **wrong** side together, fold piece in half. Weave side seams *(Fig. 7, page 35)*.

CURL (Make 2)
With Blue, cast on 20 sts.

Knit across.

Bind off all sts in **knit**, leaving a long end for sewing.

Sew one Curl to each top corner.

BASIC BEANIE

This cute, all-purpose hat has a knitted pom-pom which replaces bedraggled, clipped-end pom-poms.

⬤⬤⬤◻ INTERMEDIATE

Finished Head Circumference: {9-10-11}
{12-14-16}"/{23-25.5-28}{30.5-35.5-40.5} cm
See Sizing, page 3.

MATERIALS

Medium Weight Yarn 🧶 **MEDIUM 4**
[4 ounces, 232 yards
(113 grams, 212 meters) per skein]:
   One skein
Set of 5 double pointed knitting needles,
   size 8 (5 mm) **or** size needed for gauge
Split-ring marker
Polyester fiberfill - small amount for pom-pom
Yarn needle

GAUGE: In Stockinette Stitch
      (knit every round),
      16 sts and 24 rounds = 4" (10 cm)

Techniques used:
• Increase *(Figs. 2a & b, page 34)*
• K2 tog *(Fig. 3, page 34)*

CUFF

Cast on {36-40-44}{48-56-64} sts.

Divide sts evenly onto 4 needles *(see Using Double Pointed Needles, page 34)*.

Place a split-ring marker around the first stitch to indicate the beginning of the round *(see Markers, page 34)*.

Rnd 1: Knit around.

Rnd 2: Purl around.

Rnds 3-8: Repeat Rnds 1 and 2, 3 times.

BODY

Knit every round (Stockinette Stitch) until Body measures approximately {3-3¹/₂-4}{5-6-6¹/₂}"/ {7.5-9-10}{12.5-15-16.5} cm from cast on edge.

Sizes Preemie {Small-Medium} and Term {Medium-Large} Only
Decrease Row: Knit around decreasing {1-0} {1-4} st(s) *(see Zeros, page 34)* evenly spaced across *(see Decreasing Evenly Across, page 34)*: {35-40} {55-60} sts.

Sizes Preemie {Large} and Term {Small} Only
Increase Row: Knit around increasing {1}{2} st(s) evenly spaced across *(see Increasing Evenly Across, page 34)*: {45}{50} sts.

SHAPING

Rnd 1: (K2 tog, K3) around: {28-32-36} {40-44-48} sts.

Rnd 2: Knit around.

Rnd 3: (K2 tog, K2) around: {21-24-27} {30-33-36} sts.

Rnd 4: Knit around.

Rnd 5: (K2 tog, K1) around: {14-16-18} {20-22-24} sts.

Rnd 6: K2 tog around: {7-8-9} {10-11-12} sts.

Rnd 7: K2 tog around to last {1-0-1} {0-1-0} st(s), K {1-0-1} {0-1-0}: {4-4-5} {5-6-6} sts.

POM-POM

Rnds 1 and 2: Increase in each st around: {16-16-20} {20-24-24} sts.

Rnd 3: (K1, P1) around.

Rnd 4: (P1, K1) around.

Repeat Rnds 3 and 4, {2-2-3} {3-3-4} times.

Next Rnd: K2 tog around: {8-8-10} {10-12-12} sts.

Stuff pom pom with fiberfill.

Last Rnd: K2 tog around: {4-4-5} {5-6-6} sts.

Cut yarn leaving a long end for sewing. Thread yarn needle with long end and slip remaining stitches onto needle; gather tightly to close and secure end.

● ●

BUNNY EARS

"Some-bunny" will be adorable with long, floppy ears!

■■■■□ INTERMEDIATE

Finished Head Circumference: {9-10-11} {12-14-16}"/{23-25.5-28} {30.5-35.5-40.5} cm
See Sizing, page 3.

MATERIALS

MEDIUM **4**

Medium Weight Yarn
[3 ounces, 103 yards
(85 grams, 94 meters) per skein]:
   Pink **or** Blue - One skein
Set of 5 double pointed knitting needles,
   size 8 (5 mm) **or** size needed for gauge
Split-ring marker
Yarn needle
³/₈" (10 mm) wide washable fabric ribbon -
   18" (45.5 cm) (optional)

GAUGE: In Stockinette Stitch
         (knit every round),
         16 sts and 24 rounds = 4" (10 cm)

Techniques used
• Increase *(Figs. 2a & b, page 34)*
• K2 tog *(Fig. 3, page 34)*

Instructions continued on page 14.

13

CUFF & BODY

With Pink or Blue, work same as Cuff & Body of Basic Beanie, page 12: {4-4-5}{5-6-6} sts.

Cut yarn, leaving a long end for sewing. Thread yarn needle with end and slip remaining sts onto needle; gather tightly to close and secure end.

EAR (Make 2)

With Pink or Blue and leaving a long end for sewing, cast on {12-12-12}{14-14-14} sts.

Divide sts onto 4 needles.

Place a split-ring marker around the first stitch to indicate the beginning of the round.

Rnd 1: Knit around.

Rnd 2: Purl around.

Knit every round (Stockinette Stitch) until Ear measures {3-3-3}{4-4-4}"/(7.5-7.5-7.5) {10-10-10} cm from cast on edge.

SHAPING

Rnd 1: ★ K2 tog, K{4-4-4}{5-5-5}; repeat from ★ once **more**: {10-10-10}{12-12-12} sts.

Rnd 2: ★ K2 tog, K{3-3-3}{4-4-4}; repeat from ★ once **more**: {8-8-8}{10-10-10} sts.

Rnd 3: ★ K2 tog, K{2-2-2}{3-3-3}; repeat from ★ once **more**: {6-6-6}{8-8-8} sts.

Rnd 4: ★ K2 tog, K{1-1-1}{2-2-2}; repeat from ★ once **more**: {4-4-4}{6-6-6} sts.

Rnd 5: ★ K2 tog, K {0-0-0}{1-1-1}; repeat from ★ once **more**: {2-2-2}{4-4-4} sts.

Rnd 6: K2 tog {1-1-1}{2-2-2} time(s): {1-1-1} {2-2-2} st(s).

Term Sizes Only
Rnd 6: K2 tog: one st.

All Sizes
Cut yarn, pull end through last st on last rnd.

FINISHING

Flatten each Ear.

Thread yarn needle with long end and sew Ears to center top of Hat.

Weave ribbon around center st at front of Hat, then tie into a bow.

PERKY STRIPES

A beanie with pizzazz—this little cap steps up the cute factor a notch with a cute button finish.

◀▦▦▦▭ INTERMEDIATE

Finished Head Circumference:
{9-10-11}{12-14 16}"/{23-25.5 28}
{30.5-35.5-40.5} cm
See Sizing, page 3.

MATERIALS
Medium Weight Yarn

[4 ounces, 232 yards
(113 grams, 212 meters) per skein]:
Variegated - One skein
[5 ounces, 290 yards
(141 grams, 265 meters) per skein]:
Yellow - One skein
Set of 5 double pointed knitting needles,
size 8 (5 mm) **or** size needed for gauge
$^3/_4$" (19 mm) Buttons - 2
Yarn needle

GAUGE: In Stockinette Stitch
(knit every round),
16 sts and 24 rounds = 4" (10 cm)

Techniques used:
• Increase *(Figs. 2a & b, page 34)*
• K2 tog *(Fig. 3, page 34)*

CUFF & BODY
With Variegated, work same as Cuff & Body of Basic Beanie, page 12: {4-4-5}{5-6-6} sts.

Cut yarn, leaving a long end for sewing. Thread yarn needle with end and slip remaining sts onto needle; gather tightly to close and secure end.

FLAP (Make 2)
With Yellow and leaving a long end for sewing, cast on {8-8-8}{10-10-10} sts.

Divide sts evenly onto 4 needles.

Place a split-ring marker around the first stitch to indicate the beginning of the round.

Knit every round (Stockinette Stitch) until Flap measures approximately {3-3-4}{4-4$^1/_2$-4$^1/_2$}"/ {7.5-7.5-10}{10-11.5-11.5} cm from cast on edge.

Bind off all sts in **knit**, leaving a long end for sewing.

FINISHING
Please take caution when using pom-poms or buttons as they may present a choking hazard for infants and small children.

Thread yarn needle with long end at cast on edge of one Flap. Flatten piece and using photo as a guide, sew Flap to Hat above Cuff and $^1/_2$" (12 mm) from center front. Thread yarn needle with remaining long end and sew opposite end of Flap in place at back. Sew one button to Flap at front.
Repeat for second Flap sewing cast on edge approximately 1" (5 cm) from first Flap at center front.

RED-NOSED REINDEER

Complete with antlers and red nose that are knitted separately and stitched on, our little-Littles light the way to a special Christmas season.

▰▰▰▰▱ INTERMEDIATE

Finished Head Circumference: {9-10-11} {12-14-16}"/{23-25.5-28}{30.5-35.5-40.5} See Sizing, page 3.

MATERIALS

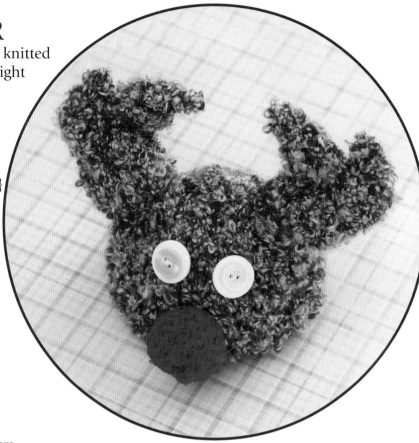

Medium Weight Yarn
[5 ounces, 245 yards
(140 grams, 224 meters) per skein]:
    Brown - One skein
[6 ounces, 335 yards
(170 grams, 306 meters) per skein]:
    Red - small amount
Set of 5 double pointed knitting needles,
    size 8 (5 mm) **or** size needed for gauge
Polyester fiberfill - small amount for Antlers
Buttons
Sewing needle and matching thread
Yarn needle

GAUGE: In Stockinette Stitch,
        (knit every round)
        16 sts and 24 rounds = 4" (10 cm)

Techniques used:
• Increase (*Figs. 2a & b, page 34*)
• K2 tog (*Fig. 3, page 34*)

CUFF & BODY

With Brown, work same as Cuff & Body of Basic Beanie, page 12: {4-4-5}{5-6-6} sts.

Cut yarn, leaving a long end for sewing. Thread yarn needle with end and slip remaining sts onto needle; gather tightly to close and secure end.

ANTLER (Make 2)
LARGE BRANCH

With Brown and leaving a long end for sewing, cast on 8 sts.

Divide sts evenly onto 4 needles.

Place a split-ring marker around the first stitch to indicate the beginning of the round.

Rnd 1: Increase in each st around: 16 sts.

Knit every round (Stockinette Stitch) until Antler measures approximately {1$^{1}/_{2}$-1$^{1}/_{2}$-1$^{1}/_{2}$} {2$^{1}/_{2}$-2$^{1}/_{2}$-2$^{1}/_{2}$}"/{4-4-4}{6.5-6.5-6.5} cm from cast on edge.

SHAPING
Row 1: K2 tog, K9, **turn**.

Row 2: P6, turn.

Row 3: K6, turn.

Row 4: P6, turn.

Begin working in rounds.

Rnd 1: K6, pick up 2 sts in end of rows (Fig. 6b, page 35), K3, K2 tog.

Rnd 2: K2 tog, K2, pick up 2 sts in end of rows, K 10, K2 tog: 16 sts.

Rnd 3: K2 tog, K 12, K2 tog: 14 sts.

Rnd 4: K2 tog, K 10, K2 tog: 12 sts.

Rnd 5: K2 tog, K8, K2 tog: 10 sts.

Rnd 6: K2 tog, K6, K2 tog: 8 sts.

Rnd 7: K2 tog, K4, K2 tog: 6 sts.

Rnd 8: K2 tog 3 times: 3 sts.

Rnd 9: K2 tog, K1: 2 sts.

Rnd 10: K2 tog: one st.

Cut yarn, pull end through last st.

SMALL BRANCH
With Brown and leaving a long end for sewing, cast on 9 sts.

Divide sts evenly onto 3 needles forming a triangle (see Using Double Pointed Needles, page 34).

Place a split-ring marker around the first stitch to indicate the beginning of the round.

Rnds 1-4: Knit around.

SHAPING

Rnd 1: K2 tog, K7: 8 sts.

Rnd 2: K2 tog, K6: 7 sts.

Rnd 3: K2 tog, K5: 6 sts.

Rnd 4: K2 tog, K4: 5 sts.

Rnd 5: K2 tog, K3: 4 sts.

Rnd 6: K2 tog twice: 2 sts.

Rnd 7: K2 tog: one st.

Cut yarn, pull end through last st.

NOSE
With Red, cast on 4 sts.

Put one st onto each of 4 needles.

Place a split-ring marker around the first stitch to indicate the beginning of the round.

Rnds 1 and 2: Increase in each st around: 16 sts.

Rnd 3: (K1, P1) around.

Rnd 4: (P1, K1) around.

Rnds 5 thru {8-8-8}{10-10-10}: Repeat Rnds 3 and 4 {2-2-2}{3-3-3} times.

Next Rnd: K2 tog around: 8 sts.

Stuff pom-pom with fiberfill.

Last Rnd: K2 tog around: 4 sts.

Cut yarn, leaving a long end for sewing. Thread yarn needle with end and slip the remaining stitches onto the needle; gather tightly and secure.

Instructions continued on page 18.

FINISHING

Please take caution when using pom-poms or buttons as they may present a choking hazard for infants and small children.

Stuff Small Branch lightly with fiberfill. Thread yarn needle with long end; sew Small Branch to Large Branch at Row 1 of Shaping. Repeat for second Small and Large Branches.

Thread yarn needle with long end. Using photo as a guide for sewing, sew Antlers to top of each side of Hat, approximately 1" (2.5 cm) from center top of Hat.

Thread yarn needle with long end. Using photo as a guide, sew Nose at center front of Hat. Using sewing needle and thread, sew buttons above Nose for eyes.

● ●

RIPPLED STRIPES

Fall colors flow together in rippled waves on this cozy beanie.

◖▬▬▭ INTERMEDIATE

Finished Head Circumference:
{9-10-11}{12-14-16}"/{23-25.5-28}
{30.5-35.5-40.5} cm
See Sizing, page 3.

MATERIALS
Medium Weight Yarn
[3.5 ounces, 170 yards
(100 grams, 156 meters) per skein]:
  Red, Lt Green, Orange, Green, **and** Brown -
  One skein **each color**
Set of 5 double pointed knitting needles,
  size 8 (5 mm) **or** size needed for gauge
Split-ring marker
Polyester fiberfill - small amount for pom-pom
Yarn needle

GAUGE: In Stockinette Stitch
     (knit every round),
     16 sts and 24 rounds = 4" (10 cm)

Techniques used:
• Increase *(Figs. 2a & b, page 34)*
• K2 tog *(Fig. 3, page 34)*

CUFF
With Red, work same as Cuff of Basic Beanie, page 12: {36-40-44}{48-56-64} sts.

BODY
Rnd 1 (Right side): With Lt Green, K2 tog {1-0-0} {0-1-0} time(s) *(see Zeros, page 34)*, knit around increasing {0-0-1}{2-0-1} sts evenly spaced around *(see Increasing Evenly Across, page 34)*: {35-40-45} {50-55-65} sts.

Rnd 2: Knit around.

Rnd 3: With Lt Green K2, with Orange K1 *(Figs. 5a & b, page 35)*, ★ with Lt Green K4, with Orange K1; repeat from ★ around to last 2 sts, with Lt Green K2.

Rnd 4: (With Lt Green K1, with Orange K1) twice, ★ with Lt Green K2, with Orange K1, with Lt Green K1, with Orange K1; repeat from ★ around to last st, with Lt Green K1; cut Lt Green.

Rnds 5 and 6: Knit around.

Rnd 7: With Orange K2, with Green K1, ★ with Orange K4, with Green K1; repeat from ★ around to last 2 sts, with Orange K2.

Rnd 8: (With Orange K1, with Green K1) twice, ★ with Orange K2, with Green K1, with Orange K1, with Green K1; repeat from ★ around to last st, with Orange K1; cut Orange.

Rnds 9 and 10: Knit around.

Rnd 11: With Green K2, with Brown K1, ★ with Green K4, with Brown K1; repeat from ★ around to last 2 sts, with Green K2.

Rnd 12: (With Green K1, with Brown K1) twice, ★ with Green K2, with Brown K1, with Green K1, with Brown K1; repeat from ★ around to last st, with Green K1; cut Green.

Knit every round (Stockinette Stitch) until piece measures approximately {3-3½-4}{5-6-6½}"/ {7.5-9-10}{12.5-15-16.5} cm from cast on edge.

Decrease Rnd: Knit around decreasing {0-0-0} {0-0-5} sts evenly spaced across *(see Decreasing Evenly Across, page 34)*: {35-40-45}{50-55-60} sts.

SHAPING
Work same as Basic Beanie: {4-5-5}{5-6-6} sts.

POM-POM
With Red, work same as Pom-pom of Basic Beanie, page 13.

TURKEY FEATHERS

The little-Little becomes his/her own crib centerpiece by donning a turkey hat with a rainbow of fall colors. Sure to make most adults chuckle, and great for blackmail pictures later on in the "teen years."

▬▬▬▬▭ INTERMEDIATE

Finished Head Circumference:
{9-10-11}{12-14-16}"/{23-25.5-28}
{30.5-35.5-40.5} cm
See Sizing, page 3.

MATERIALS

Medium Weight Yarn
[3.5 ounces, 170 yards
(100 grams, 156 meters) per skein]:
    Brown, Beige, Red, Orange, Green **and**
    Lt Green - One skein **each** color
Set of 5 double pointed knitting needles,
    size 8 (5 mm) **or** size needed for gauge
10 mm Pom-poms - 2 for eyes
Sewing needle and matching thread
Yarn needle

GAUGE: In Stockinette Stitch
        (knit every round),
        16 sts and 24 rounds = 4" (10 cm)

Techniques used:
• Increase *(Figs. 2a & b, page 34)*
• K2 tog *(Fig. 3, page 34)*

CUFF & BODY

With Brown, work same as Cuff & Body of Basic Beanie, page 12: {4-4-5}{5-6-6} sts.

Cut yarn, leaving a long end for sewing. Thread yarn needle with end and slip remaining sts onto needle; gather tightly to close and secure end.

FEATHER (Make 5)

Make one **each** with Beige, Red, Orange, Green, and Lt Green.

Leaving a long end for sewing, cast on {10-10-10}{12-12-12} sts.

Divide sts onto 3 needles forming a triangle *(see Using Double Pointed Needles, page 34)*.

Place a split-ring marker around the first stitch to indicate the beginning of the round.

Rnd 1: Knit around.

Rnd 2: Purl around.

Rnd 3: Knit around.

Repeat Rnd 3 until Feather measures approximately {2¹/₂-2¹/₂-2¹/₂}{3¹/₂-3¹/₂-3¹/₂}"/{6.5-6.5-6.5}{9-9-9} cm.

SHAPING

Rnd 1: ★ K2 tog, K{3-3-3}{4-4-4}; repeat from ★ once **more**: {8-8-8}{10-10-10} sts.

Rnd 2: ★ K2 tog, K{2-2-2}{3-3-3}; repeat from ★ once **more**: {6-6-6}{8-8-8} sts.

Rnd 3: ★ K2 tog, K{1-1-1}{2-2-2}; repeat from ★ once **more**: {4-4-4}{6-6-6} sts.

Rnd 4: ★ K2 tog, K{0-0-0}{1-1-1}; repeat from ★ once **more**: {2-2-2}{4-4-4} sts.

Rnd 5: K2 tog around: {1-1-1}{2-2-2} st(s).

Term Sizes Only
Rnd 6: K2 tog around: one st.

All Sizes
Cut yarn, pull yarn end through last st.

BEAK

With Beige and leaving a long end for sewing, cast on 4 sts.

Divide sts onto 3 needles forming a triangle.

Place a split-ring marker around the first stitch to indicate the beginning of the round.

Rnd 1 (Right side): Knit around.

Rnd 2: Purl around.

Rnd 3: Knit around.

Rnd 4: K2 tog around: 2 sts.

Rnd 5: K2 tog: one st.

Cut yarn, pull end through last st.

WATTLE

With Red and leaving a long end for sewing, cast on 2 sts.

Rows 1 and 2: Increase in each st across: 8 sts.

Bind off all sts in **knit**.

FINISHING

Please take caution when using pom-poms or buttons as they may present a choking hazard for infants and small children.

Thread yarn needle with long end on one Feather. Flatten Feather and using photo as a guide for placement, sew Feather to top of Hat. Repeat for remaining Feathers.

Thread yarn needle with long end on Beak; using photo as a guide for placement, sew Beak to center front of Hat, approximately 2" (5 cm) up from cast on edge. Thread yarn needle with long end on Waddle; sew Wattle to Hat below Beak.

With sewing needle and matching thread, sew pom-poms above Beak for eyes.

INDEPENDENCE DAY

Red, White, and Blue in the NICU (and beyond).
Vertical stripes "flag" our patriotic babies.

◼◼◼◻ INTERMEDIATE

Finished Head Circumference:
{9-10-11}{12-14-16}"/{23-25.5-28}
{30.5-35.5-40.5} cm
See Sizing, page 3.

MATERIALS

Medium Weight Yarn 〔MEDIUM 4〕
[6 ounces, 335 yards
(170 grams, 306 meters) per skein]:
 Red, White, **and** Blue - One skein
 each color
Set of 5 double pointed knitting needles,
 size 8 (5 mm) **or** size needed for gauge
Split-ring marker
Polyester fiberfill - small amount for pom-pom
Yarn needle

GAUGE: In Stockinette Stitch,
 (knit every round)
 16 sts and 24 rounds = 4" (10 cm)

Techniques used:
• Increase *(Figs. 2a & b, page 34)*
• K2 tog *(Fig. 3, page 34)*

CUFF

With Blue, cast on {36-40-44}{48-56-64} sts.

Divide sts evenly onto 4 needles *(see Using Double Pointed Needles, page 34)*.

Place a split-ring marker around the first stitch to indicate the beginning of the round *(see Markers, page 34)*.

Rnd 1: Knit around.

Rnd 2: Purl around.

Rnds 3 and 4: Knit around.

Rnds 5 and 6: ★ With Blue K2, with White K2 *(Figs. 5a & b, page 35)*; repeat from ★ around.

Rnds 7 and 8: (With White K2, with Blue K2) around.

Cut White.

Rnds 9 and 10: Knit around.

Rnd 11: Purl around.

Cut Blue.

BODY

Rnd 1: (With Red K2, with White K2) around.

Repeat Rnd 1 for pattern until piece measures approximately {3-3¹/₂-4}{5-6-6¹/₂}"/{7.5-9-10}{12.5-15-16.5} cm from cast on edge.

SHAPING

Rnd 1: (With Red K2, With White K2 tog) around: {27-30-33}{36-42-48} sts.

Rnd 2: (With Red K2, with White K1) around.

Rnd 3: (With Red K2 tog, with White K1) around: {18-20-22}{24-28-32} sts.

Rnd 4: (With Red K1, with White K1) around; cut Red.

Rnd 5: K2 tog around: {9-10-11}{12-14-16} sts.

Rnd 6: K {1-0-1}{0-0-0}, K2 tog around *(see Zeros, page 34)*: {5-5-6}{6-7-8} sts.

Sizes Term {Small-Medium-Large}
Rnd 7: K2 tog {1-2-2} time(s), knit around: {5-5-6} sts.

All Sizes
Cut White.

POM-POM

Rnds 1 and 2: With Red, increase in each st around: {20-20-24}{20-20-24} sts.

Rnd 3: (K1, P1) around.

Rnd 4: (P1, K1) around.

Repeat Rnds 3 and 4, {2-2-3}{3-3-4} times.

Next Rnd: K2 tog around: {10-10-12}{10-10-12} sts.

Stuff pom-pom with fiberfill.

Last Rnd: K2 tog around: {5-5-6}{5-5-6} sts.

Cut yarn, leaving a long end for sewing. Thread yarn needle with end and slip remaining sts onto needle; gather tightly to close and secure end.

BASIC CONE

The quintessential skating-style hat forms the basis for sprightly winter caps, including Santa hats for Christmas.

■■■□ INTERMEDIATE

Finished Head Circumference: {9-10-11} {12-14-16}"/{23-25.5-28}{30.5-35.5-40.5} cm
See Sizing, page 3.

MATERIALS
Medium Weight Yarn **MEDIUM 4**
[4 ounces, 232 yards
(113 grams, 212 meters) per skein]:
    One skein
Set of 5 double pointed knitting needles,
    size 8 (5 mm) **or** size needed for gauge
Polyester fiberfill - small amount for pom-pom
Yarn needle

GAUGE: In Stockinette Stitch
            (knit every round),
            16 sts and 24 rounds = 4" (10 cm)

Techniques used:
• Increase *(Figs. 2a & b, page 34)*
• K2 tog *(Fig. 3, page 34)*

CUFF
Cast on {36-40-44}{48-56-64} sts.

Divide sts evenly onto 4 needles *(see Using Double Pointed Needles, page 34)*.

Place a split-ring marker around the first stitch to indicate the beginning of the round *(see Markers, page 34)*.

Rnd 1: Knit around.

Rnd 2: Purl around.

Rnds 3-8: Repeat Rnds 1 and 2, 3 times.

BODY
Knit every round (Stockinette Stitch) until Body measures approximately {3-3-3}{4-4-4}"/
{7.5-7.5-7.5}{10-10-10} cm from cast on edge.

**Sizes Preemie {Small-Medium} &
Term {Medium-Large} Only
Decrease Row:** Knit around decreasing {1-0}
{1-4} st(s) *(see Zeros, page 34)* evenly spaced across *(see Decreasing Evenly Across, page 34)*: {35-40}
{55-60} sts.

**Sizes Preemie Large & Term Small Only
Increase Row:** Knit around increasing {1}{2} st(s) evenly spaced across *(see Increasing Evenly Across, page 34)*: {45}{50} sts.

SHAPING
Size Term Large Only
Rnd 1: (K2 tog, K 10) around: 55 sts.

Rnds 2-6: Knit around.

Rnd 7: (K2 tog, K9) around: 50 sts.

Rnds 8-12: Knit around.

Rnd 13: (K2 tog, K8) around: 45 sts.

Rnds 14-18: Knit around.

Rnd 19: (K2 tog, K7) around: 40 sts.

Rnds 20-24: Knit around.

Rnd 25: (K2 tog, K6) around: 35 sts.

Rnds 26-30: Knit around.

Rnd 31: (K2 tog, K5) around: 30 sts.

Rnds 32-36: Knit around.

Rnd 37. (K2 tog, K4) around. 25 sts.

Rnds 38-42: Knit around.

Rnd 43: (K2 tog, K3) around: 20 sts.

Rnds 44-48: Knit around.

Rnd 49: (K2 tog, K2) around: 15 sts.

Rnds 50 54: Knit around.

Rnd 55: (K2 tog, K1) around: 10 sts.

Rnds 56-60: Knit around.

Rnd 61: K2 tog around: 5 sts.

Size Term Medium Only
Work same as size Term Large beginning with Rnd 7: 5 sts.

Size Term Small Only
Work same as size Term Large beginning with Rnd 13: 5 sts.

Size Preemie Large Only
Work Rnds same as size Term Large beginning with Rnd 19: 5 sts.

Size Preemie Medium Size Only
Work same as size Term Large beginning with Rnd 25: 5 sts.

Size Preemie Small Size Only
Work same as size Term Large beginning with Rnd 31: 5 sts.

POM-POM

Rnds 1 and 2: Increase in each st around: 20 sts.

Rnd 3: (K1, P1) around.

Rnd 4: (P1, K1) around.

Repeat Rnds 3 and 4, {2-2-3}{3-3-4} times.

Next Rnd: K2 tog around: 10 sts.

Stuff Pom-pom with fiberfill.

Last Rnd: K2 tog around: 5 sts.

Cut yarn, leaving a long end for sewing. Thread yarn needle with end and slip remaining stitches onto needle; gather tightly to close and secure end.

SANTA

A soft floppy Santa hat, perfect for baby's first Christmas.

◼◼◼◻ **INTERMEDIATE**

Finished Head Circumference:
{9-10-11}{12-14-16}"/{23-25.5-28}
{30.5-35.5-40.5} cm
See Sizing, page 3.

MATERIALS **MEDIUM 4**
Medium Weight Yarn
[6 ounces, 315 yards
(170 grams, 288 meters) per skein]:
White **and** Red - One skein **each** color
Set of 5 double pointed knitting needles,
size 8 (5 mm) **or** size needed for gauge
Polyester fiberfill - small amount for pom-pom
Yarn needle

GAUGE: In Stockinette Stitch
(knit every round),
18 sts and 24 rounds = 4" (10 cm)

Techniques used:
• Increase *(Figs. 2a & b, page 34)*
• K2 tog *(Fig. 3, page 34)*

CUFF
With White, work same as Cuff of Basic Cone, page 24.

BODY
With Red, work same as Body of Basic Cone.

POM-POM
With White, work same as Pom-pom of Basic Cone.

SANTA'S ELVES

A celebratory hat for all Santa's elves, knitted in 100% cotton.

▬▬▬▬▬▭ INTERMEDIATE

Finished Head Circumference:

{9-10-11}{12-14-16}"/{23-25.5-28}
{30.5-35.5-40.5} cm
See Sizing, page 3.

MATERIALS

100% Cotton Medium Weight Yarn MEDIUM ④
[2.5 ounces, 120 yards
(71 grams, 109 meters) per skein]:
   Ecru - One skein
[2 ounces, 95 yards
(56 grams, 86 meters) per skein]:
   Variegated - One skein
Set of 5 double pointed knitting needles,
   size 8 (5 mm) **or** size needed for gauge
Polyester fiberfill - small amount for pom-pom
Yarn needle

GAUGE: In Stockinette Stitch
   (knit every round),
   18 sts and 24 rounds = 4" (10 cm)

Techniques used:

• Increase *(Figs. 2a & b, page 34)*
• K2 tog *(Fig. 3, page 34)*

CUFF

With Ecru, work same as Cuff of Basic Cone, page 24.

BODY

With Variegated, work same as Body of Basic Cone: 5 sts.

Cut Variegated.

POM-POM

With Ecru, work same as Pom-pom of Basic Cone.

SANTA'S ELFIN STRIPES
Santa's Little Helpers need hats too!

▰▰▰▱ INTERMEDIATE

Finished Head Circumference:
{9-10-11}{12-14-16}"/{23-25.5-28}
{30.5-35.5-40.5} cm
See Sizing, page 3.

MATERIALS
Medium Weight Yarn **4**
[6 ounces, 315 yards
(170 grams, 288 meters) per skein]:
White **and** Red - One skein **each** color
[5 ounces, 250 yards
(140 grams, 229 meters) per skein]:
Green - One skein
Set of 5 double pointed knitting needles,
size 8 (5 mm) **or** size needed for gauge
Polyester fiberfill - small amount for pom-pom
Yarn needle

GAUGE: In Stockinette Stitch (knit every round),
18 sts and 24 rounds = 4" (10 cm)

Techniques used:
• Increase *(Figs. 2a & b, page 34)*
• K2 tog *(Fig. 3, page 34)*

CUFF
With White, work same as Cuff of Basic Cone,
page 24.

BODY
Alternating 2 rounds Red and 2 rounds Green,
knit every rnd until Body measures approximately
{3-3-3}{4-4-4}"/{7.5-7.5-7.5}{10-10-10} cm from
cast on edge.

SHAPING
Maintaining stripe pattern throughout, work same
as Basic Cone: 5 sts.

Cut Red and Green.

POM-POM
With White, work same as Pom-pom of Basic Cone.

PUNKIN' PATCH HAT

Modified ribbing creates the ridges for a little Punkin's punkin patch hat.

Finished Head Circumference:
{9 10 11}{12 14 16}"/{23 25.5 28}
{30.5-35.5-40.5} cm
See Sizing, page 3.

MATERIALS

Medium Weight Yarn
[3.5 ounces, 170 yards
(100 grams, 156 meters) per skein]:
 Orange, Green, **and** Lt Green - One skein
 each color
Set of 5 double pointed knitting needles,
 size 8 (5 mm) **or** size needed for gauge
Split-ring marker
Yarn needle

GAUGE: In Stockinette Stitch
 (knit every round),
 16 sts and 24 rounds = 4" (10 cm)
 In pattern (not stretched),
 15 sts = 2¹/₂" (6.25 cm)

Techniques used:
• Increase (*Figs. 2a & b, page 34*)
• K2 tog (*Fig. 3, page 34*)
• P2 tog (*Fig. 4, page 35*)

BODY

With Orange, cast on {40-45-50}{55-60-65} sts.

Divide sts evenly onto 4 needles (*see Using Double Pointed Needles, page 34*).

Place a split-ring marker around the first stitch to indicate the beginning of the round (*see Markers, page 34*).

Rnd 1: (K3, P2) around.

Repeat Rnd 1 until Body measures approximately {3-3¹/₂-4}{5-6-6¹/₂}"/{7.5-9-10}{12.5-15-16.5} cm from cast on edge.

SHAPING

Rnd 1: K1, with Green K1 (*Figs. 5a & b, page 35*), ★ with Orange K1, P2, K1, with Green K1; repeat from ★ around to last 3 sts, with Orange K1, P2.

Rnd 2: ★ With Green K3, with Orange P2; repeat from ★ around; cut Orange.

Rnd 3: (K3, P2 tog) around: {32-36-40} {44-48-52} sts.

Rnd 4: (K2, K2 tog) around: {24-27-30} {33-36-39} sts.

Rnd 5: (K2 tog, K1) around: {16-18-20}{22-24-26} sts.

Rnd 6: K2 tog around: {8-9-10}{11-12-13} sts.

Rnd 7: K {0-1-0}{1-0-1} (*see Zeros, page 34*), K2 tog around; slip remaining sts onto one double pointed needle: {4-5-5}{6-6-7} sts.

Instructions continued on page 30.

STEM

Rows 1-8: Knit across, do **not** turn; slide sts to opposite end of needle.

Bind off all sts in **knit**.

LEAF

With Lt Green and leaving a long end for sewing, cast on 3 sts.

Row 1 (Right side): Increase, K1, increase: 5 sts.

Row 2: K2, P1, K2.

Row 3: Increase, K3, increase: 7 sts.

Row 4: K3, P1, K3.

Row 5: Knit across.

Rows 6-11: Repeat Rows 4 and 5, 3 times.

Row 12: K2 tog, K3, K2 tog: 5 sts.

Row 13: K2, P1, K2.

Row 14: K2 tog, K1, K2 tog: 3 sts.

Row 15: K1, P1, K1.

Row 16: K2 tog, K1: 2 sts.

Row 17: K2 tog: one st.

Cut yarn, pull end through last st. Thread yarn needle with long end from cast on, using photo as a guide for placement, sew Leaf at base of Stem.

TENDRIL

With Lt Green, cast 12 sts.

Row 1: Increase in each st across: 24 sts.

Bind off all sts in **knit**, leaving a long end for sewing.

Thread yarn needle with long end. Using photo as a guide for placement, sew Tendril at base of Stem by Leaf.

• •

WHICH WITCH

This is a girlie purple witch hat with black buckle and flared brim.

▣▣▣▣▢ INTERMEDIATE

Finished Head Circumference:
{9-10-11}{12-14-16}"/{23-25.5-28}
{30.5-35.5-40.5} cm
See Sizing, page 3.

MATERIALS
Medium Weight Yarn 【MEDIUM 4】
[7 ounces, 355 yards
(199 grams, 325 meters) per skein]:
     Purple **and** Black - One skein **each** color
Set of 5 double pointed knitting needles,
     size 8 (5 mm) **or** size needed for gauge
Yarn needle

GAUGE: In Stockinette Stitch
          (knit every round),
          16 sts and 24 rounds = 4" (10 cm)

Techniques used:
• Increase *(Figs. 2a & b, page 34)*
• K2 tog *(Fig. 3, page 34)*

BRIM

With Purple, cast on {72-80-88}{96-112-128} sts.

Divide sts evenly onto 4 needles *(see Using Double Pointed Needles, page 34)*.

Place a split-ring marker around the first stitch to indicate the beginning of the round *(see Markers, page 34)*.

Rnd 1: Knit around.

Rnd 2: Purl around.

Rnd 3-6: Knit around.

BODY
Rnd 1: K2 tog around: {36-40-44} {48-56-64} sts

Rnds 2-4: Knit around.

Cut Purple.

Rnds 5-9: With Black, knit around.

Cut Black.

With Purple, knit every round (Stockinette Stitch) until piece measures approximately {4-4-4}{5-5-5}"/{10-10-10} {12.5-12.5-12.5} cm from cast on edge.

Sizes Preemie {Small-Medium} & Term {Medium-Large} Only
Decrease Row: Knit around decreasing {1-0} {1-4} sts *(see Zeros, page 34)* evenly spaced across *(see Decreasing Evenly Across, page 34)*: {35-40} {55-60} sts.

Sizes Preemie Large & Small Only
Increase Row: Knit around increasing {1}{2} sts evenly spaced across *(see Increasing Evenly Across, page 34)*: {45}{50} sts.

SHAPING
Size Term Large Only
Rnd 1: (K2 tog, K 10) around: 55 sts.

Rnds 2 and 3: Knit around.

Rnd 4: (K2 tog, K9) around: 50 sts.

Rnds 5 and 6: Knit around.

Rnd 7: (K2 tog, K8) around: 45 sts.

Rnds 8 and 9: Knit around.

Rnd 10: (K2 tog, K7) around: 40 sts.

Rnds 11 and 12: Knit around.

Rnd 13: (K2 tog, K6) around: 35 sts.

Rnds 14 and 15: Knit around.

Rnd 16: (K2 tog, K5) around: 30 sts.

Rnds 17 and 18: Knit around.

Rnd 19: (K2 tog, K4) around: 25 sts.

Rnds 20 and 21: Knit around.

Rnd 22: (K2 tog, K3) around: 20 sts.

Rnds 23 and 24: Knit around.

Rnd 25: (K2 tog, K2) around: 15 sts.

Rnds 26 and 27: Knit around.

Rnd 28: (K2 tog, K1) around: 10 sts.

Instructions continued on page 32.

Rnds 29 and 30: Knit around.

Rnd 31: K2 tog around: 5 sts.

Cut yarn, leaving a long end for sewing. Thread yarn needle with end and slip remaining sts onto needle; gather tightly to close and secure end.

Size Term Medium Only
Complete same as size Term Large beginning with Rnd 4: 5 sts.

Size Term Small Only
Complete same as size Term Large beginning with Rnd 7: 5 sts.

Size Preemie Large Only
Complete same as size Term Large beginning with Rnd 10: 5 sts.

Size Preemie Medium Only
Complete same as size Term Large beginning with Rnd 13: 5 sts.

Size Preemie Small Only
Complete same as size Term Large beginning with Rnd 16: 5 sts.

BUCKLE
With Black and using chart, duplicate stitch a Buckle to center front of Hat *(Figs. A & B)*.

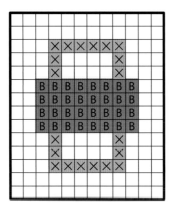

DUPLICATE STITCH
Duplicate Stitch is worked on Stockinette Stitch. Each knit stitch forms a V and you want to completely cover that V, so that the design appears to have been knit into the Hat. Each square on a chart represents one knit stitch that is to be covered by a Duplicate Stitch.

Thread a yarn needle with an 18" (45.5 cm) length of yarn. Beginning at lower right of a design and with right side facing, bring the needle up from the wrong side at the base of the V, leaving an end to be woven in later (never tie knots). The needle should always go between the strands of yarn. Follow the right side of the V up and insert the needle from right to left under the legs of the V immediately above it, keeping the yarn on top of the stitch *(Fig. A)*, and draw through. Follow the left side of the V back down to the base and insert the needle back through the bottom of the same stitch where the first stitch began *(Fig. B, Duplicate Stitch completed)*.

Continuing to follow chart, bring needle up through the next stitch. Repeat for each stitch, keeping tension even with tension of knit fabric to avoid puckering.

When a length of yarn is finished, run it under several stitches on back of work to secure.

Fig. A

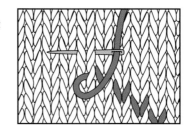

Fig. B

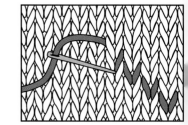

ABBREVIATIONS

cm	centimeters
K	knit
kg	kilograms
lb(s)	pound(s)
mm	millimeters
P	purl
Rnd(s)	Round(s)
st(s)	stitch(es)
tog	together

★ — work instructions following ★ as many **more** times as indicated in addition to the first time.

( ) or [ ] — work enclosed instructions **as many** times as specified by the number immediately following **or** work all enclosed instructions in the stitch or space indicated **or** contains explanatory remarks.

colon (:) — the number(s) given after a colon at the end of a row or round denote(s) the number of stitches you should have on that row or round.

GAUGE

Exact gauge is **essential** for proper size. Before beginning your project, make a sample swatch in the yarn and needle specified in the individual instructions. After completing the swatch, measure it, counting your stitches and rows or rounds carefully. If your swatch is larger or smaller than specified, **make another, changing needle size to get the correct gauge**. Keep trying until you find the size needles that will give you the specified gauge.

KNIT TERMINOLOGY	
UNITED STATES	**INTERNATIONAL**
gauge =	tension
bind off =	cast off
yarn over (YO) =	yarn forward (yfwd) **or** yarn around needle (yrn)

KNITTING NEEDLES		
UNITED STATES	**ENGLISH U.K.**	**METRIC (mm)**
0	13	2
1	12	2.25
2	11	2.75
3	10	3.25
4	9	3.5
5	8	3.75
6	7	4
7	6	4.5
8	5	5
9	4	5.5
10	3	6
10½	2	6.5
11	1	8
13	00	9
15	000	10
17	---	12.75

Yarn Weight Symbol & Names	LACE 0	SUPER FINE 1	FINE 2	LIGHT 3	MEDIUM 4	BULKY 5	SUPER BULKY 6
Type of Yarns in Category	Fingering, size 10 crochet thread	Sock, Fingering, Baby	Sport, Baby	DK, Light Worsted	Worsted, Afghan, Aran	Chunky, Craft, Rug	Bulky, Roving
Knit Gauge Range* in Stockinette St to 4" (10 cm)	33-40** sts	27-32 sts	23-26 sts	21-24 sts	16-20 sts	12-15 sts	6-11 sts
Advised Needle Size Range	000-1	1 to 3	3 to 5	5 to 7	7 to 9	9 to 11	11 and larger

*GUIDELINES ONLY: The chart above reflects the most commonly used gauges and needle sizes for specific yarn categories.

** Lace weight yarns are usually knitted on larger needles to create lacy openwork patterns. Accordingly, a gauge range is difficult to determine. Always follow the gauge stated in your pattern.

●□□□ BEGINNER	Projects for first-time knitters using basic knit and purl stitches. Minimal shaping.
●●□□ EASY	Projects using basic stitches, repetitive stitch patterns, simple color changes, and simple shaping and finishing.
●●●□ INTERMEDIATE	Projects with a variety of stitches, such as basic cables and lace, simple intarsia, double-pointed needles and knitting in the round needle techniques, mid-level shaping and finishing.
●●●● EXPERIENCED	Projects using advanced techniques and stitches, such as short rows, fair isle, more intricate intarsia, cables, lace patterns, and numerous color changes.

MARKERS

When using double pointed needles, a split-ring marker is placed around the first stitch of the round to indicate the beginning of a round.

Place a marker as instructed and move it up at the beginning of each round.

ZEROS

To consolidate the length of an involved pattern, zeros are sometimes used so that all sizes can be combined. For example, increase every sixth row 5{1-0} time(s) means the first size would increase 5 times, the second size would increase once, and the largest size would do nothing.

USING DOUBLE POINTED NEEDLES

The stitches are divided evenly between three *(Fig. 1a)* or four double pointed needles as specified in the individual pattern. Form a triangle *(Fig. 1b)* or a square *(Fig. 1c)*.

Do not twist cast on edge. With the remaining needle, work across the stitches on the first needle. You will now have an empty needle with which to knit the stitches from the next needle. Work the first stitch of each needle firmly to prevent gaps.

Fig. 1a

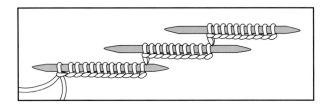

Fig. 1b

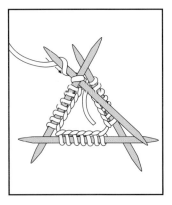

Fig. 1c

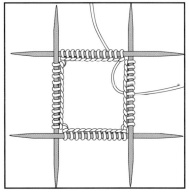

INCREASING OR DECREASING EVENLY ACROSS

Add one to the number of increases/decreases required and divide that number into the number of stitches on the needle. Subtract one from the result and the new number is the approximate number of stitches to be worked between each increase/decrease. Adjust the number as needed.

INCREASE

The increase in this book uses one stitch to make two stitches. You will have two stitches on the right needle for the one stitch worked off the left needle.

Knit the next stitch but do **not** slip the old stitch off the left needle *(Fig. 2a)*. Insert the right needle into the **back** loop of the **same** stitch and knit it *(Fig. 2b)*, then slip the old stitch off the left needle.

Fig. 2a

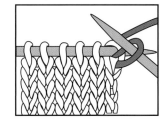

Fig. 2b

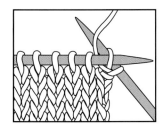

KNIT 2 TOGETHER
(abbreviated K2 tog)

Insert the right needle into the **front** of the first two stitches on the left needle as if to **knit** *(Fig. 3)*, then **knit** them together as if they were one stitch.

Fig. 3

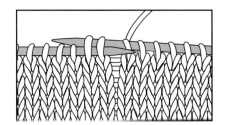

PURL 2 TOGETHER
(abbreviated P2 tog)

Insert the right needle into the **front** of the first two stitches on the left needle as if to **purl** *(Fig. 4)*, then purl them together as if they were one stitch.

Fig. 4

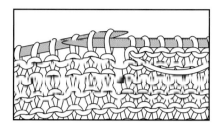

CHANGING COLORS

When changing colors, always pick up the new color from **beneath** the dropped yarn and keep the color which has just been worked to the left *(Fig. 5a)*. This will prevent holes in the finished piece. Carry the unused yarn loosely along the back *(Fig. 5b)*. Take extra care to keep your tension even.

Fig. 5a

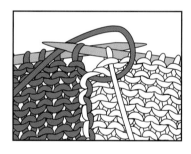

Fig. 5b

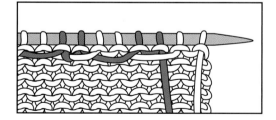

PICKING UP STITCHES

When instructed to pick up stitches, insert the needle as shown below. Put the yarn around the needle as if to *purl (Fig. 6a)* or as if to *knit (Fig. 6b)*, then bring the needle with the yarn back through the stitch, resulting in a stitch on the needle. Repeat this along the edge, picking up the required number of stitches.

A crochet hook may be helpful to pull yarn through.

Fig. 6a   Fig. 6b

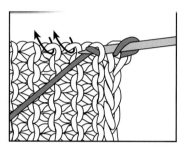 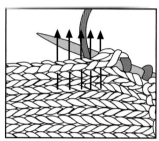

WEAVING SEAMS

With the **right** side of both pieces facing you and edges even, sew through both sides once to secure the seam. Insert the needle under the bar **between** the first and second stitches on the row and pull the yarn through *(Fig. 7)*. Insert the needle under the next bar on the second side. Repeat from side to side, being careful to match rows. If the edges are different lengths, it may be necessary to insert the needle under two bars at one edge.

Fig. 7

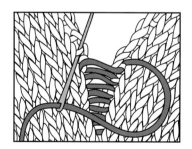

35

BASIC SKILLS
SLINGSHOT CAST ON

Step 1: Pull a length of yarn from the skein, allowing approximately 1" (2.5 cm) of yarn for each stitch to be cast on. Make a slip knot at the measured distance, pulling gently on both yarn ends to tighten stitch on needle.

Step 2: Hold the needle in your right hand with your index finger resting on the slip knot.

Step 3: Place the short end of the yarn over your left thumb, and bring the working yarn up and over your left index finger. Hold both yarn ends in your left palm with your 3 remaining fingers *(Fig. 8a)*.

Fig. 8a

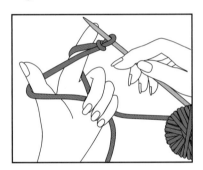

Step 4: Insert the tip of the needle **under** the first strand of yarn on your left thumb *(Fig. 8b)*.

Fig. 8b

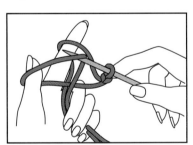

Step 5: Bring the needle **over** and around the first strand on your index finger *(Fig. 8c)*.

Fig. 8c

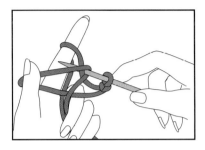

Step 6: Pull the yarn and needle down through the loop on your thumb *(Fig. 8d)*.

Fig. 8d

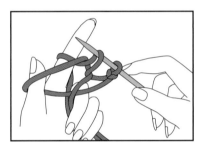

Step 7: Slip your thumb out of the loop and bring it toward you, catching the yarn end to form a new loop on your thumb *(Fig. 8e)*, and gently pulling to tighten the new stitch on the needle. Rest your index finger on the new stitch.

Fig. 8e

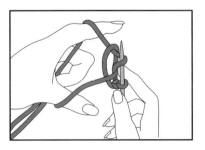

Repeat Steps 4-7 for each additional stitch.

ENGLISH METHOD

THE KNIT STITCH

Step 1: Hold the needle with the stitches in your left hand and the empty needle in your right hand.

Step 2: With the working yarn in **back** of the needles, insert the right needle into the stitch closest to the tip of the left needle as shown in Fig. 9a.

Fig. 9a

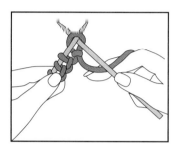

Step 3: Hold the right needle with your left thumb and index finger while you bring the yarn beneath the right needle and between the needles from **back** to **front** *(Fig. 9b)*.

Fig. 9b

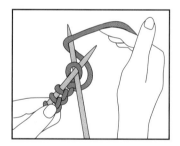

Step 4: With your right hand, bring the right needle (with the loop of yarn) toward you and through the stitch *(Figs. 9c & d)*, slip the old stitch off the left needle and gently pull to tighten the new stitch on the shaft of the right needle.

Fig. 9c

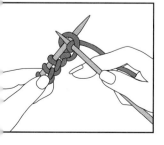

Fig. 9d

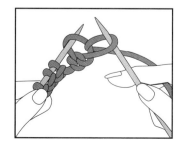

THE PURL STITCH

Step 1: Hold the needle with the stitches in your left hand and the empty needle in your right hand.

Step 2: With the yarn in **front** of the needles, insert the right needle into the front of the stitch as shown in Fig. 10a.

Fig. 10a

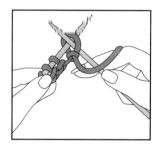

Step 3: Hold the right needle with your left thumb and index finger while you bring the yarn **between** the needles from **right** to **left** and around the right needle *(Fig. 10b)*.

Fig. 10b

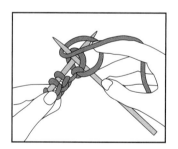

Step 4: Move the right needle (with the loop of yarn) through the stitch and away from you *(Fig. 10c)*, slip the old stitch off the left needle and gently pull to tighten the new stitch on the shaft of the right needle.

Fig. 10c

CONTINENTAL METHOD
THE KNIT STITCH

Step 1: Hold the needle with the stitches in your left hand and the empty needle in your right hand. Loop the working yarn over the index finger of your left hand and hold it loosely across the palm of your hand with your little finger.

Step 2: With the yarn in **back** of the needles, insert the right needle into the stitch closest to the tip of the left needle as shown in Fig. 11a.

Fig. 11a

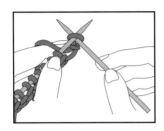

Step 3: With your left index finger, bring the yarn between the needles from **left** to **right** *(Fig. 11b)*.

Fig. 11b

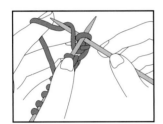

Step 4: With your right hand, bring the right needle (with the loop of yarn) toward you and through the stitch *(Figs. 11c & d)*, slip the old stitch off the left needle and gently pull to tighten the new stitch on the shaft of the right needle.

Fig. 11c

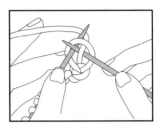

Fig. 11d

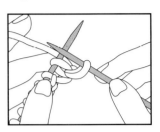

THE PURL STITCH

Step 1: Hold the needle with the stitches in your left hand and the empty needle in your right hand.

Step 2: With the yarn in **front** of the needles, insert the right needle into the front of the stitch as shown in Fig. 12a.

Fig. 12a

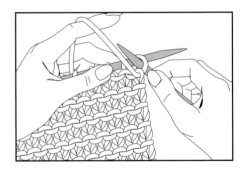

Step 3: With your index finger, bring the yarn **between** the needles from **right** to **left** around the right needle *(Fig. 12b)*.

Fig. 12b

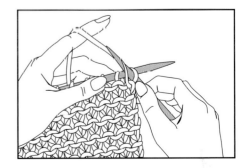

Step 4: Move your left index finger forward while moving the right needle (with the loop of yarn) through the stitch and away from you *(Fig. 12c)*, slip the old stitch off the left needle and gently pull to tighten the new stitch on the shaft of the right needle.

Fig. 12c

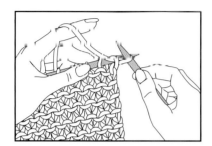

BIND OFF

Binding off is the method used to remove and secure your stitches from the knitting needles so that they don't unravel.

Work the first two stitches.

Use your left needle as a tool to lift the back stitch on the right needle up and over the front stitch *(Fig. 13a)* and completely off the right needle *(Fig. 13b)*. Don't forget to remove the left needle from the stitch.

You now have one stitch on your right needle and you have bound off one stitch. Count the stitch as you bind it off, not as you work it.

Work the next stitch; you will have two stitches on your right needle. Bind off as before.

Continue until your left needle is empty and there is only one stitch left on your right needle.

Cut the yarn leaving a long end to hide later.

Slip the stitch off the right needle, pull the end through the stitch *(Fig. 13c)* and tighten the stitch.

Fig. 13a

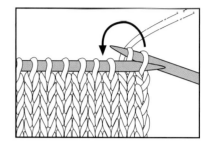

Fig. 13b

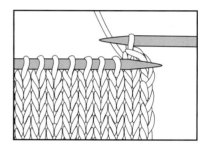

Fig. 13c

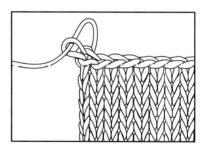

YARN INFORMATION

Each Hat in this leaflet was made using Medium Weight Yarn. Any brand of Medium Weight Yarn may be used. It is best to refer to the yardage/meters when determining how many balls or skeins to purchase. Remember, to arrive at the finished size, it is the GAUGE/TENSION that is important, not the brand of yarn.
For your convenience, listed below are the specific yarns used to create our photography models.

BASIC PAPER BAG
Red Heart® Kids™
#2930 Crayon

HAVE A HEART
TLC® Amoré™
Ecru - #3105 Light Cream
Red - #3907 Red Velvet

POSEY
Baby Bee™ Dreamy Baby Chenille (page 7)
Purple - #60 Sugarplum
Pink - #40 Boo Pink
Green - #30 Froggy
Lion Brand® Vanna's Choice® (page 6)
Purple - #146 Dusty Purple
Pink - #101 Pink
Green - #173 Dusty Green

BASIC JESTER
Red Heart® Kids™
#2930 Crayon

LITTLE FRANKIE STEIN
I Love This Yarn!
Black - #30 Black
Green - #788 Limelight
Orange - #232 Orange

SPRINGY CURLS
Bernat® Cottontots™
White - #90005 Wonder White
Blue - #90129 Blue Berry

BASIC BEANIE
Red Heart® Kids™
#2930 Crayon

BUNNY EARS
Lion Brand® Nature's Choice Organic® Cotton
Blue - #108 Dusty Blue
Lion Brand® Vanna's Choice®
Pink - #101 Pink

PERKY STRIPES
Red Heart® Kids™
Variegated - #2945 Bikini
Yellow - #2230 Yellow

RED-NOSED REINDEER
Yarn Bee™ Bouclé Traditions
Brown - #135 Brown Mix
TLC® Amoré™
Red - #3907 Red Velvet

RIPPLED STRIPES
Lion Brand® Vanna's Choice®
Red - #133 Brick
Lt Green - #173 Dusty Green
Orange - #135 Rust
Green - #174 Olive
Brown - #126 Chocolate

TURKEY FEATHERS
Lion Brand® Vanna's Choice®
Brown - #126 Chocolate
Beige - #123 Beige
Red - #133 Brick
Orange - #135 Rust
Green - #174 Olive
Lt Green - #173 Dusty Green

INDEPENDENCE DAY
TLC® Amoré
Red - #3907 Red Velvet
White - #3105 Light Cream
Blue - #3823 Lake Blue

BASIC CONE
Red Heart® Kids™
#2930 Crayon

SANTA
Caron® Simply Soft®
Red - #9730 Autumn Red
White - #9701 White

SANTA'S ELVES
Lily® Sugar 'n Cream® Stripes
Variegated - #21532 Holiday Stripes
Lily® Sugar 'n Cream®
Ecru - #00004 Soft Ecru

SANTA'S ELFIN STRIPES
Caron® Simply Soft®
White - #9701 White
Red - #9730 Autumn Red
Caron® Simply Soft® Heather
Green - #9503 Woodland Heather

PUNKIN' PATCH
Lion Brand® Vanna's Choice®
Orange - #135 Rust
Green - #174 Olive
Lt Green - #173 Dusty Green

WHICH WITCH
I Love This Yarn!
Purple - #280 Periwinkle
Black - #30 Black